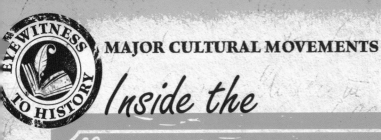

EYEWITNESS TO HISTORY

MAJOR CULTURAL MOVEMENTS

Inside the

NATIVE AMERICAN RIGHTS MOVEMENT

This is INDIAN LAND

By
Theresa
Morlock

Gareth Stevens
PUBLISHING

Please visit our website, www.garethstevens.com. For a free color catalog of all our high-quality books, call toll free 1-800-542-2595 or fax 1-877-542-2596.

Library of Congress Cataloging-in-Publication Data

Names: Morlock, Theresa, author.
Title: Inside the Native American rights movement / Theresa Morlock.
Description: New York : Gareth Stevens Publishing, [2018] | Series:
  Eyewitness to history: Major cultural movements | Includes index.
Identifiers: LCCN 2017025565| ISBN 9781538211496 (pbk.) | ISBN 9781538211502 (6 pack) | ISBN 9781538211519 (library bound)
Subjects: LCSH: Indians of North America–Government relations–Juvenile
  literature. | Indians of North America–Civil rights–Juvenile literature.
  | Indians of North America–Legal status, laws, etc.–Juvenile literature.
Classification: LCC E93 .M85 2018 | DDC 323.1197–dc23
LC record available at https://lccn.loc.gov/2017025565

First Edition

Published in 2018 by
Gareth Stevens Publishing
111 East 14th Street, Suite 349
New York, NY 10003

Designer: Katelyn E. Reynolds
Editor: Therese Shea

Photo credits: Cover, pp. 1, 21 Bettmann/Getty Images; cover, p. 1 (background image) Michael D. Sullivan/MPI/Getty Images; cover, p. 1 (logo quill icon) Seamartini Graphics Media/Shutterstock.com; cover, p. 1 (logo stamp) YasnaTen/Shutterstock.com; cover, p. 1 (color grunge frame) DmitryPrudnichenko/Shutterstock.com; cover, pp. 1-32 (paper background) Nella/Shutterstock.com; cover, pp. 1-32 (decorative elements) Ozerina Anna/Shutterstock.com; pp. 1-32 (wood texture) Reinhold Leitner/Shutterstock.com; pp. 1-32 (open book background) Elena Schweitzer/Shutterstock.com; pp. 1-32 (bookmark) Robert Adrian Hillman/Shutterstock.com; p. 5 Justin Sullivan/Getty Images; p. 7 O.S. Goff/Hulton Archive/Getty Images; p. 9 Ben Nolan (cosmictraveler photoblog on Flickr)/Wikipedia.org; pp. 11, 15 © CORBIS/Corbis via Getty Images; p. 13 U.S. National Archives and Records Administration/Wikipedia.org; p. 17 Ernst Haas/Getty Images; p. 19 Ralph Crane/The LIFE Picture Collection/Getty Images; p. 23 Peter Davis/Getty Images; p. 25 © Wally McNamee/CORBIS/Corbis via Getty Images; p. 27 Carl Iwasaki/The LIFE Images Collection/Getty Images; p. 28 Michael Nigro/Pacific Press/LightRocket/Getty Images.

Printed in the United States of America

CPSIA compliance information: Batch #CW18GS: For further information contact Gareth Stevens, New York, New York at 1-800-542-2595.

CONTENTS

*Words in the glossary appear in **bold** type the first time they are used in the text.*

WHO ARE THE
Native Americans?

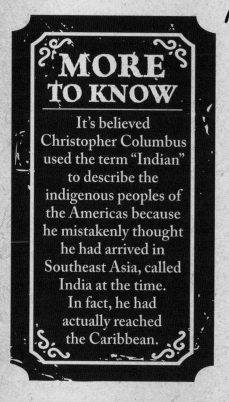

MORE TO KNOW

It's believed Christopher Columbus used the term "Indian" to describe the indigenous peoples of the Americas because he mistakenly thought he had arrived in Southeast Asia, called India at the time. In fact, he had actually reached the Caribbean.

The name "Native American" is commonly used to describe the original peoples of North America and their descendants. Native Americans have been referred to by other names, too, including Indians and American Indians. But all these labels are used to describe thousands of different indigenous, or native, nations of varying languages, religions, and **cultures**. That's why many people dislike reducing the many indigenous groups to a single term.

The ancestors of modern Native Americans created flourishing civilizations that prospered until the arrival of European explorers and settlers. Since the European invasion, Native Americans have suffered mistreatment, cultural destruction, and even **genocide**. However, in spite of generations of **oppression**, Native American peoples continue to endure, taking pride in their cultures and fighting for their futures.

The struggle for Native American rights is ongoing. In this picture, taken in 2017, a protester demanding rights for his people stands outside the White House in Washington, DC.

WE EXIST

WE RESIST

WE RISE

NATIVE AMERICAN OR AMERICAN INDIAN?

Lakota **activist** Russell Means once stated: *"I abhor [hate] the term Native American."* Means preferred the term "American Indian." He appreciated that this label is the only cultural title in which the word "American" comes first. Means considered native peoples to be *"prisoners"* of the US government and said that "Native American" is a *"government term used to describe all the indigenous prisoners of the United States."*

5

A HISTORY
of Injustice

MANIFEST DESTINY

Westward expansion during the 1800s was partly inspired by the belief in an idea called manifest destiny. Manifest destiny stressed that white Americans were superior to native peoples. Americans who believed in manifest destiny thought it was their right to spread their own culture across the country. Manifest destiny had serious consequences for Native Americans, who were forced to leave their lands to make way for white settlers.

When Europeans first arrived in North America, there were as many as 16 million native people living there. The newcomers believed themselves to be superior to the Native Americans they encountered and entitled to the land and all its resources—even though the indigenous peoples had lived there for thousands of years. The Europeans also brought diseases for which the Native Americans had no immunity. These illnesses wiped out huge numbers of native communities.

As the newly formed United States expanded during the 1800s, the government put policies in place to relocate Native Americans. Native American nations were driven from their homelands and forced onto areas of land called reservations.

In some states, whole Native American communities were slaughtered. In others, Native Americans were legally enslaved.

Sitting Bull was a Sioux chief who resisted oppression in the late 1800s. He stated: "If we must die . . . we die defending our rights."

MORE TO KNOW

In 1830, President Andrew Jackson signed the Indian Removal Act to pressure Native Americans to move west of the Mississippi River. In 1838 and 1839, thousands of Cherokee were forcibly marched west, an event known as the Trail of Tears that resulted in the death of over 4,000 Native Americans.

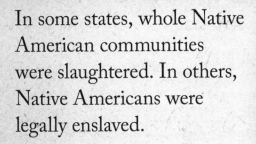

Broken TREATIES

Throughout the late 18th and early 19th centuries, treaties with Native Americans established rules about territory boundaries and interactions between native peoples and the government. Some treaties ceded, or surrendered, Native American land to the US government in exchange for supplies or peace. Unfortunately, the United States didn't uphold many promises. In some cases, land that was pledged to the Native Americans in treaties was later seized.

Modern Native Americans continue to feel the consequences of these broken treaties. Suzan Shown Harjo, a member of the Cheyenne and Hodulgee

SHIFTING ATTITUDES

The treaties ratified between 1774 and 1832 recognized Native American territory as foreign lands. Non-Indians were expected to carry special identification to enter these territories. However, treaties between 1832 and 1871 addressed native nations as part of and dependent on the United States. The Supreme Court said Native Americans were like children under a guardian. In 1871, Congress passed the Indian Appropriations Act. It said native peoples weren't recognized as independent nations anymore, so no treaties were necessary.

Muscogee Indian nations, stated in 2015: *"They aren't just the Indians' treaties. No one gave us anything. No one was dragging any land behind them when they came here. This was our land."*

About 374 treaties were ratified, or approved, between the United States and native peoples. The monument pictured here remembers the Treaty of Canandaigua of 1794, one of the earliest agreements between a native nation and the United States.

THE LAST GENERAL COUNCIL OF THE UNITED STATES WITH THE IROQUOIS CONFEDERACY WAS HELD IN CANANDAIGUA AND THE RESULTANT TREATY WAS SIGNED NOVEMBER 11, 1794, BY U.S. AGENT TIMOTHY PICKERING

SACHEMS AND WARRIORS
FARMER'S BROTHER, CORNPLANTER, RED JACKET, LITTLE BEARD, FISH CARRIER, LITTLE BILLY, HEAP OF DOGS, HANDSOME LAKE, HALF TOWN, AND FIFTY OTHERS

WITNESSES
ISRAEL CHAPIN, JAMES SMEDLY, AUGUSTUS PORTER, WILLIAM EWING AND OTHERS

INTERPRETERS
HORATIO JONES, JOSEPH SMITH, JASPER PARRISH

1902

FORCED *Assimilation*

BOARDING SCHOOLS

Boarding schools were created to separate Native American children from their parents and the lessons they'd learn from their elders. Esther Burnett Horne, a Shoshone teacher, described her school experience: *"Indian people were taught that their culture was backward and uncivilized."* The children were taught English and encouraged to forget their native languages. They were also taught trades. Boarding schools forced children to dress and behave like white people and even abandon their religion.

The US government took several actions during the late 1800s with the goal of dividing Native American people and forcing them to **assimilate** to white culture. The Dawes General Allotment Act of 1887 distributed pieces of reservation land among individuals. The Native Americans who received land would become US citizens, were subject to the same laws as white citizens, and were expected to farm their private property. These divisions and expectations undermined the cultural unity of many Native American communities.

Most efforts for assimilation were fueled by **racist** ideas. By forcing Native Americans to abandon their traditions, white Americans suggested that traditional Native American lifestyles were "savage" and Native Americans could only lead successful lives if they adopted "civilized" white culture.

This photograph shows children at a boarding school in Kickapoo, Kansas. Traditionally, most Native American cultures didn't have written languages. Instead, elders educated children through storytelling.

A TIME
of Change

Native Americans were granted American citizenship in 1924. However, even as legal citizens, laws **discriminated** against them. For example, some states created tests and poll taxes that made it difficult for Native Americans with little education or low incomes to vote.

In 1934, the Indian Reorganization Act was passed, signaling a change in attitude toward native peoples. This law encouraged native groups to be self-governed so they might recover aspects of their traditional societies. Over 170 groups accepted the Indian Reorganization Act and established councils. About 80 other groups rejected it, believing the federal government shouldn't interfere further.

In 1944, the National Congress of American Indians (NCAI), an assembly of 100 Native American leaders, first gathered to discuss federal policies and **advocate** for Native American peoples.

The photo above shows the representatives of the National Congress of American Indians in 1944. The NCAI, the oldest and largest representative Native American organization, is still active today.

NATIVE AMERICAN SOLDIERS

In part, citizenship was granted to Native Americans in recognition of their service during World War I. About 17,000 Native Americans served in the US military during that war. In 1940, Congress passed the Nationality Act, which confirmed their American citizenship. During World War II, about 25,000 Native Americans served in the military. Navajo and Comanche "code talkers" played a key role in the war by passing on secret information in their native languages.

MORE TO KNOW

The mission of the National Congress of American Indians is to protect the rights of Native Americans, improve the quality of life of native communities, and maintain traditions for future generations.

FIGHTING *Back*

TERMINATION POLICY

During the 1950s, the US Congress created what was called a "termination policy" toward Native Americans. This policy worked toward disbanding Native American groups so that Native Americans could become "true" American citizens. Conditions on reservations were extremely poor, and Congress maintained that Native Americans would overcome poverty by fully assimilating to white American culture, even moving to urban areas. Over 100 native groups were terminated between 1953 and 1964.

Historically, Native Americans resisted oppression with uprisings and battles against the US government. However, the modern Native American rights movement, born in the 1960s, took a different approach. Activists began to call the American public's attention to the poor conditions in which many Native Americans were living. The main focuses of activism were unemployment, bad housing, and lack of healthcare.

In 1965, the Voting Rights Act was passed. This act helped eliminate obstacles that prevented Native Americans from voting. In 1968, the Indian Civil Rights Act was passed *"to ensure that the American*

Indian is afforded the broad constitutional rights secured to other Americans."

However, this measure was divisive as it allowed the federal government to interfere with native governments' decisions.

ROAD CLOSED

This INDIA LAND

INDI POW

In this photo, Native American men protest over fishing rights in the Columbia River, which flows through the state of Washington. Protests were a way for Native Americans to draw public notice to their issues.

The AMERICAN INDIAN *Movement*

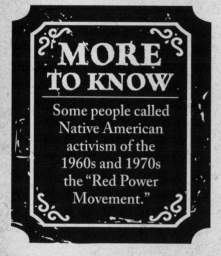

MORE TO KNOW

Some people called Native American activism of the 1960s and 1970s the "Red Power Movement."

In 1968, the American Indian Movement, or AIM, was founded in Minneapolis, Minnesota. At first, the activist organization focused on addressing the needs of Native Americans living in urban poverty. Later, the group's concerns expanded to protecting civil rights, establishing economic independence, controlling native territory, restoring lands, and renewing traditional culture.

Lakota activist Russell Means became a leading spokesperson for AIM. Means reflected, *"Before AIM, Indians were dispirited, defeated, and culturally dissolving. . . . We put Indians and Indian rights smack dab in the middle of the public consciousness for the first time since the so-called Indian wars."* AIM organized protests and demonstrations to make the public fully aware of the injustices that Native Americans suffered.

AIM played a leading role in the Native American civil rights activism of the 1960s and 1970s. Its members sometimes employed extreme methods to gain national attention and gather support for their causes.

BACK TO TRADITIONS

Some Native American activists of the 1960s and 1970s emphasized a return to traditionalism, which meant valuing Native American culture by practicing the traditions of their ancestors, communicating in native languages, and rediscovering traditional religions. To do this, activists had to resist social pressure to turn their backs on their culture. Instead, they proudly claimed their identities as Native American people and reconnected themselves with their ancestral history.

OCCUPATION
of Alcatraz

In 1970, President Richard Nixon declared that the US government would adopt a new policy toward Native American nations. This policy was called "self-determination," and it rejected the earlier government strategy of "termination." Under this new plan, Nixon declared that *"the Indian future is determined by Indian acts and Indian decisions."* Nixon's self-determination policy was intended to show Native American leaders the concerns of activists were heard.

On November 20, 1969, a group called the Indians of All Tribes, or IAT, staged a demonstration to reclaim Alcatraz Island in San Francisco Bay. In a letter, the IAT wrote, *"We, the native Americans, reclaim the land known as Alcatraz Island in the name of all American Indians by right of discovery,"* meaning that Alcatraz belonged to the Native Americans because they were the first to actually discover it.

The letter offered to buy Alcatraz *"for 24 dollars in glass beads and red cloth, a precedent [example] set by the white man's purchase of a similar island about 300 years ago."* The writers drew parallels between Alcatraz's limited resources and reservation conditions. The IAT held Alcatraz until June 11, 1971, when the US government forcibly removed the remaining activists.

The occupation of Alcatraz, a former prison built on the island, successfully called attention to Native American demands for the return of illegally taken lands. Writing on the walls still remains from the protest.

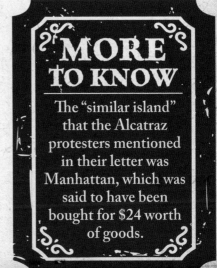

MORE TO KNOW

The "similar island" that the Alcatraz protesters mentioned in their letter was Manhattan, which was said to have been bought for $24 worth of goods.

THE TRAIL
of Broken Treaties

In 1972, AIM organized a cross-country protest to call attention to issues surrounding Native American rights. It was called the Trail of Broken Treaties. Over 600 people took part in the protest, which began in Saint Paul, Minnesota, and ended at the US Bureau of Indian Affairs in Washington, DC. The protesters occupied the Bureau of Indian Affairs for a week.

Assiniboine activist Hank Adams wrote the 20-Point Position Paper, which outlined AIM's goals, demands for government action, and a plan for future interactions between native nations and the US government. AIM stated: *"We go [to Washington] because America has been only too ready to express shame, and suffer none from the expression—while remaining wholly unwilling to change to allow life for Indian people."*

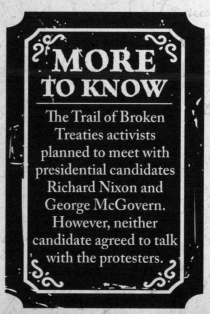

MORE TO KNOW

The Trail of Broken Treaties activists planned to meet with presidential candidates Richard Nixon and George McGovern. However, neither candidate agreed to talk with the protesters.

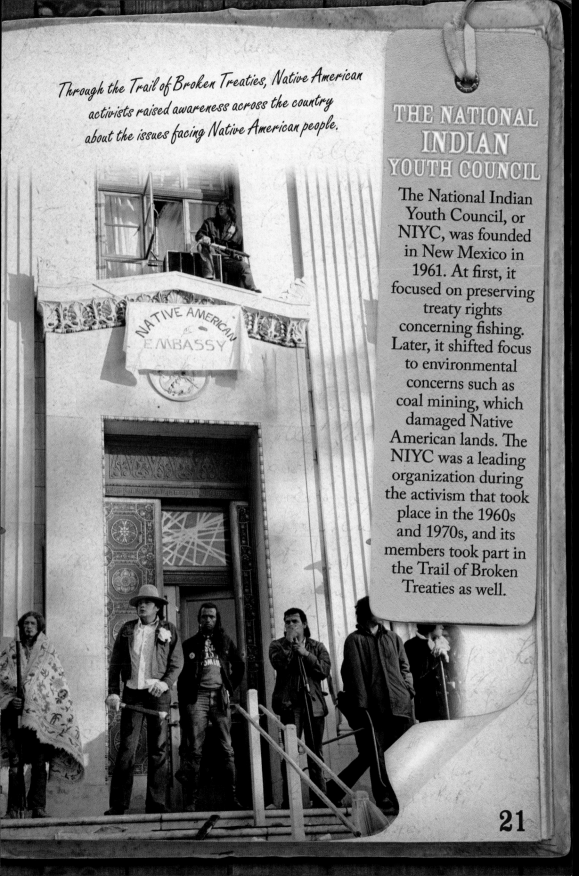

Through the Trail of Broken Treaties, Native American activists raised awareness across the country about the issues facing Native American people.

NATIVE AMERICAN EMBASSY

THE NATIONAL INDIAN YOUTH COUNCIL

The National Indian Youth Council, or NIYC, was founded in New Mexico in 1961. At first, it focused on preserving treaty rights concerning fishing. Later, it shifted focus to environmental concerns such as coal mining, which damaged Native American lands. The NIYC was a leading organization during the activism that took place in the 1960s and 1970s, and its members took part in the Trail of Broken Treaties as well.

WOUNDED *Knee*

RICHARD WILSON

The 1973 Wounded Knee protest was partly inspired by complaints about Richard Wilson, chairman of the Oglala Lakota (Sioux) on the Pine Ridge Reservation. Many Oglala Lakota thought that Wilson, who supported assimilation, was dishonest. They believed he had turned against his people and favored the US government to serve his own interests. Oglala Lakota and AIM members banded together to demand that Wilson step down. He eventually lost his seat and moved from the reservation.

In February 1973, AIM members organized an occupation of Wounded Knee, a site on the Pine Ridge Reservation in South Dakota. In 1890, the US Army attacked and killed more than 200 Sioux men, women, and children there. At the time of the occupation in 1973, Wounded Knee had some of the worst living conditions in the nation. Activists took **hostages** and demanded that the US government improve reservation conditions and honor treaty agreements with Native American nations.

Violence broke out between activists and federal agents, resulting in the death of two Sioux. One activist later reported, "*They were shooting machine-gun fire at us, tracers coming in at us at nighttime just like a war zone.*" AIM held control of Wounded Knee for 71 days.

Activists surrendered control of Wounded Knee on May 8, 1973. In the years that followed the occupation of the site, reservation conditions continued to grow worse.

MORE TO KNOW

Today, conditions on the Pine Ridge Reservation continue to be poor. Between 70 and 80 percent of adults on the reservation are unemployed. The county is one of the poorest in the United States.

THE LONGEST *Walk*

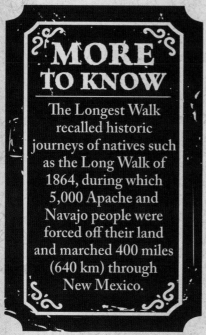

MORE TO KNOW

The Longest Walk recalled historic journeys of natives such as the Long Walk of 1864, during which 5,000 Apache and Navajo people were forced off their land and marched 400 miles (640 km) through New Mexico.

In February 1978, Native American activists traveled 3,000 miles (4,800 km) from San Francisco, California, to Washington, DC. The march came to be called the "Longest Walk." It was a response to new bills proposed by Congress, which would infringe on, or disregard, Native American land and water rights and limit native powers. The protest symbolized the long marches that Native Americans were forced to take when they were driven from their traditional homelands. Over 2,000 activists participated, some even walking the entire distance. The journey lasted 5 months.

AIM cofounder Dennis Banks reflected on activism in the 1970s like the Longest Walk, stating: *"Americans realized that native people are still here, that they have a moral standing, a legal standing."*

When Native American activists arrived in Washington, DC, they took part in 12 days of protests. The Longest Walk was successful—Congress didn't pass the bills.

THE BLACK HILLS LAND CLAIM

Under the Treaty of Fort Laramie of 1868, the Black Hills territory was promised to the Sioux Nation. In 1877, however, the US government seized the territory from the Sioux. In 1980, a case was brought before the US Supreme Court to return the land. The Supreme Court offered the Sioux $17.5 million in payment. The Sioux refused to accept the money because the land was never for sale. They continue to demand the Black Hills.

25

FORWARD STEPS,
Backward Steps

OFFENSIVE MASCOTS

Sports **mascots** are another target of Native American activists. Professional athletic teams such as the Washington Redskins, Cleveland Indians, and Atlanta Braves use Native American mascots. Many Native Americans are pushing to change these symbols. The #notyourmascot movement opposes the use of racist mascots. Although a mascot might seem harmless to a non-Native American, mascots support untrue ideas about native cultures and promote disrespect for their history.

Native Americans continued to struggle to overcome social and economic oppression throughout the 1980s, 1990s, and into the 21st century. In 1988, the Supreme Court permitted a road to be built through a sacred Native American site in California. In 1991, the court passed a ruling that said states could deny unemployment benefits to people who used **peyote** during religious ceremonies. Many believed both rulings infringed on Native American religious freedom. These decisions represented setbacks to the civil rights advances made during the 1970s.

Racist attitudes, poverty, and educational and economic opportunities are still issues today. Activist John Trudell stated:

"There have been some positive

things that have happened for the tribes, but it's a constant, vigilant [watchful] fight about protecting what resources we have in terms of land and rights."

In 1994, the religious use of peyote was legalized, but the fight for the rights to certain sacred sites still continues.

MORE TO KNOW

Cultural sensitivity is an important part of the Native American rights movement. Respect is the first step toward building a better future.

WE EXIST,
We Resist

The Native American civil rights movement is far from over. The protest against the Dakota Access Pipeline, or DAPL, has brought the ongoing battle into the public eye once again. This underground oil pipeline runs through lands near the Standing Rock Sioux's reservation and its water supply. Its construction threatens to pollute water resources and has already caused damage to areas of cultural importance to the Sioux.

The Standing Rock Sioux and members of over 200 other native groups gathered together in 2016 to resist the pipeline and protect land and resources, stating: *"The Standing Rock movement is bigger than one tribe. It has evolved into a powerful global phenomenon [experience] highlighting the necessity to respect Indigenous Nations and their right to protect their homelands, environment, and future generations."*

TIMELINE
KEY MOMENTS IN THE HISTORY OF NATIVE AMERICAN RIGHTS

1832 — The Supreme Court establishes that the Cherokee are a sovereign nation.

1838 — The Cherokee are forced to march west of the Mississippi River during the Trail of Tears.

1887 — Congress passes the Dawes General Allotment Act, which divides native lands.

1934 — The Indian Reorganization Act replaces the Dawes Act and encourages native groups to be self-governed.

1944 — The National Congress of American Indians is founded.

1953 — Native groups begin to be disbanded under a policy passed by US Congress.

1968 — The American Indian Movement (AIM) is established.

1969 — Native American activists begin an occupation of Alcatraz Island.

1970 — President Richard Nixon adopts a "self-determination" policy toward Native Americans.

1972 — The Trail of Broken Treaties protest begins, and activists occupy the Bureau of Indian Affairs.

1973 — AIM members occupy Wounded Knee for 71 days.

1978 — The Longest Walk protest march takes place.

1990 — President George H. W. Bush establishes November as Native American Indian Heritage Month.

2008 — About 800 Native Americans repeat the Longest Walk march.

2016 — Protesters gather in Standing Rock, North Dakota, to stop the construction of the Dakota Access Pipeline near the reservation.

OVERCOMING CHALLENGES

Today, some of the main concerns of Native American activists include identity and assimilation, sovereignty, reviving traditional culture, economic development, and healthcare. Many groups are taking steps to teach native languages and traditions to promote unity. **Casinos** and other businesses have been built to create economic opportunities for people living on reservations. Health issues such as alcoholism and diabetes are being addressed to create healthier conditions for young Native American people.

29

GLOSSARY

activist: a person who uses or supports strong actions to help make changes in politics or society

advocate: to speak in support of

assimilate: to adopt the ways of another culture

casino: a building used for gambling

culture: the beliefs, arts, and ways of life of a particular society

discriminate: to treat a person unfairly just because he or she is different

genocide: the killing of all the people from a national, ethnic, or religious group, or an attempt to do this

hostage: a person taken by force to secure the taker's demands

mascot: a person, animal, or object adopted by a group as a symbolic figure

nomadic: describing people who move from place to place instead of living in one place all the time

oppression: treating people in a cruel or unfair way

peyote: a drug from the peyote cactus traditionally used in religious rituals and celebrations

racist: poor treatment of or violence against people because of their race. Also, the belief that some races of people are better than others.

FOR MORE
Information

Books

Blomquist, Katie. *American Indians in the 1800s: Right and Resistance*. Huntington Beach, CA: Teacher Created Materials, 2017.

Johnson, Troy. *Red Power: The Native American Civil Rights Movement*. New York, NY: Chelsea House, 2007.

Machajewski, Sarah. *American Indian Rights Movement*. New York, NY: PowerKids Press, 2017.

Websites

Civil Rights 101: Native Americans
www.civilrights.org/resources/civilrights101/native.html
This site offers readers insight into Native American civil rights activism.

Indian Country Diaries: Today's Challenges
www.pbs.org/indiancountry/challenges/
Find more in-depth information on challenges facing Native Americans today.

Native Voices
www.nlm.nih.gov/nativevoices/exhibition/index.html
Explore the history and cultural life of Native Americans, including a timeline and interviews.

INDEX